A **TRUE** BOOK™

The Maryland Colony

KEVIN CUNNINGHAM

Children's Press®
An Imprint of Scholastic Inc.
New York Toronto London Auckland Sydney
Mexico City New Delhi Hong Kong
Danbury, Connecticut

Content Consultant
Jeffrey Kaja, PhD
Associate Professor of History
California State University, Northridge

Library of Congress Cataloging-in-Publication Data

Cunningham, Kevin, 1966–
    The Maryland Colony/Kevin Cunningham.
        p. cm.—(A true book)
    Includes bibliographical references and index.
    ISBN-13: 978-0-531-25390-8 (lib. bdg.)   ISBN-13: 978-0-531-26603-8 (pbk.)
    ISBN-10: 0-531-25390-2 (lib. bdg.)   ISBN-10: 0-531-26603-6 (pbk.)
    1. Maryland—History—Colonial period, ca. 1600–1775—Juvenile literature. I. Title. II. Series.
    F184.C87 2011
    975.2'02—dc22   2011008914

Find the Truth!

Everything you are about to read is true *except* for one of the sentences on this page.

Which one is **TRUE**?

T or F Slavery was illegal in Maryland.

T or F Tobacco was a major crop in colonial Maryland.

Find the answers in this book.

Contents

Margaret Brent

4

Tobacco was a major cash crop in colonial Maryland.

THE **BIG** TRUTH!

Maryland's Founding Fathers

How did these founders serve the United States and the cause of independence? **40**

The Maryland Toleration Act of 1649

Timeline of Maryland Colony History

1000 C.E.

Native people speaking Algonquian languages begin to depend on agriculture.

1524

Explorer Giovanni da Verrazano lands on the North American coast.

1634

Cecilius and Leonard Calvert found Maryland.

1776

Maryland colonial troops fight in the Battle of Long Island.

1788

Maryland approves the U.S. Constitution.

CHAPTER 1

The Native Americans

Native Americans sharing the **Algonquian** languages settled in Maryland centuries before Europeans colonized the area. They lived near water they called Chesapeake, meaning the "great shellfish bay." Dome-shaped houses were grouped in small villages. They had relied on agriculture as a main source of food since about 1000 C.E. Women planted crops such as maize (corn), beans, and squash. The Algonquian also grew tobacco. They smoked it during religious gatherings. They also used it as medicine.

Hunting and Fishing

The Algonquian hunted deer and other game in nearby forests. Animals provided meat for food. They also provided furs and skins for clothes and bones for tools. The Algonquian also netted and speared seafood such as oysters and turtles. They made dugout canoes by scraping out the core of burned trees. The canoes could be as long as 20 feet (6.1 meters). They were up to 4 feet (1.2 m) wide.

Algonquian fished for bluegill, rockfish, northern pike, and other fish in the area's waters.

Verrazano was born in Italy but worked for France.

Strangers Offshore

Europeans became aware of the region no later than 1524. Italian explorer Giovanni da Verrazano sailed to North America that year. He passed by Chesapeake Bay on the Atlantic Coast but continued to sail north. Verrazano did not stay. But soon other Europeans came. Some native groups offered the use of their land to the settlers. Organized trade developed with the newcomers. Europeans continued to arrive.

PENNSYLVANIA

Appalachian Mountains

Delaware River

Fort Cumberland □

S U S Q U E H A N N O C K

Susquehanna River

NEW JERSEY

Frederick Town •

VIRGINIA

Potomac River

Baltimore •

Patuxent River

Kent Island

Annapolis •

P I S C A T A W A Y

DELAWARE

Delaware Bay

MARYLAND

N A N T I C O K E

St. Clement's Bay
St. Clement's Island

St. Mary's City •

Chesapeake Bay

0	miles	50
0	km	50

——— Colonial boundaries
- - - Present boundaries

A T L A N T I C   O C E A N

Area
enlarged

Original
13 Colonies

CHAPTER 2

Lord Baltimore's Colony

European countries claimed North American land throughout the 1500s. Businessmen and settlers saw the new region as an opportunity to make money. Beaver fur was particularly valuable. Europeans founded colonies to trade with Native Americans who trapped beaver. The fur was made into hats and other fine clothing for rich Europeans. Settlers gave the Indians items such as guns, metal pots, and axes in return for the fur.

The success of the fur trade kept the Kent Island trading post busy.

The Fur Trade

Englishman William Claiborne built a trading post on Kent Island in Chesapeake Bay in 1631. Claiborne already had a successful fur-trading business in the nearby English colony of Virginia. About 100 colonists quickly settled on Kent Island. English businessmen soon wanted to establish more businesses in the region. George Calvert was also known as Lord Baltimore. He asked England's King Charles I for a **charter** to set up a colony named Maryland.

The Maryland Colony

Calvert died before the charter took effect. His son Cecilius was the second Lord Baltimore. Cecilius continued his father's work. Cecilius's brother Leonard bought land from the Yaocomaco Indians in 1634 for a settlement called St. Mary's City. The colonists planted maize and other Indian crops with the natives' help. The settlers also began planting tobacco. They hoped to turn it into a profitable **cash crop**.

Historic St. Mary's City can still be visited today.

St. Mary's City served as Maryland's capital until 1695.

Troubled Beginnings

Neighboring Virginia disliked the new Maryland Colony. Calvert's charter had allowed him to take Kent Island from Claiborne, a Virginian. The two colonies also competed for furs. Calvert was Catholic. But Virginians were Protestants, or non-Catholic Christians. The two groups disliked one another. But the Calverts brought Catholic and Protestant settlers to Maryland. They hoped the two faiths could live in peace with one another and with Native Americans.

St. Ignatius Catholic Church was founded in 1641 by one of the first Maryland settlers.

Maryland's law guaranteeing religious freedom became known as the Toleration Act.

Claiborne attacked St. Mary's City in 1635. The colonies battled two more times in the 1640s. Cecilius Calvert appointed a Protestant governor to lead Maryland. He hoped this would bring peace. The colony's **legislature** passed a law that allowed all Maryland Christians to worship as they pleased. The system worked until Protestant Marylanders successfully seized power in the colony in 1688. They soon outlawed Catholicism.

Tobacco Plantations

Tobacco became a valuable cash crop. Most people grew it on small plots of land. But some wealthy growers established large farms called plantations. One of the growers' problems was finding enough people to work in the fields. Maryland's small population was not growing quickly. Few children were being born there. Few women had settled in the colony. This meant there were few mothers. Men outnumbered women about three to one.

Tobacco is still grown in the St. Mary's area today.

An overseer watches as two slaves work on a Maryland plantation.

Tobacco growers paid **indentured servants**
to come to Maryland to work the plantations.
Indentured servants worked several years to repay
a planter for paying their way to America. But fewer
people chose to be indentured servants after 1670.
Plantation owners began bringing in slaves from the
Caribbean and Virginia. Maryland's slave population
numbered about 8,000 by 1715. This was about one-
third of the colony's total population.

CHAPTER 3

Life in Maryland

Maryland farmers lived a hard life. Men, women, and children rose before dawn to do their chores. They often worked until the evening hours. Tobacco quickly drained the soil of nutrients. Farmers were often forced to move to new fields. Maryland's wet summers allowed disease-carrying mosquitoes to breed beyond control. Disease killed so many settlers in the colony's early days that most did not live past age 40.

 By the 1700s, colonial families were larger, with more children to help with chores.

Expensive Land, Cheap Land

Wooden houses eventually replaced the one-room log cabins of the early settlement period. The wealthy built large houses. But most Marylanders were not rich. Many rented their farms from plantation owners because they could not afford to buy land. Low tobacco prices forced farmers to turn to growing crops such as maize by the 1680s. Cheap land soon lured people to an area of Maryland's frontier called the Piedmont.

A log cabin was built from the trees cut down when farmland was cleared.

Colonial women prepared wool and spun it into yarn. They then wove the yarn into cloth.

Women on the Farm

Maryland began to attract female **immigrants** as the 1600s continued. Most married farmers. Their children grew up and married. This added to Maryland's population. Women raised the families. They cooked and cleaned the house. They also kept gardens and mended clothes. Women began making and selling a variety of homemade products as the population increased. These included yarn spun from wool and butter churned from milk.

Large tobacco plantations required many people to work on them.

Men on the Farm

Men cleared the land and plowed the soil. They also planted and harvested. A typical farmer used wooden tools and plows that were sometimes edged with iron. Metal tools later became more common. Men and children tended pigs, cattle, and chickens. But many Maryland men were becoming tradesmen by the late 1600s.

Margaret Brent

Margaret Brent came from a wealthy Catholic family. Unlike most women in Maryland, she owned property. She managed her land and lent money to settlers. She also convinced workers to join the colony. Brent made sure local soldiers who were owed money got fed and paid after Leonard Calvert died. Brent was an important citizen. But the Maryland government refused to let her vote or run for office because she was a woman.

Brent is remembered as the first woman in North America to request the right to vote.

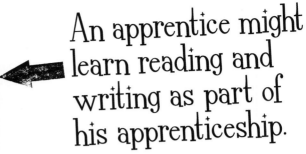
An apprentice might learn reading and writing as part of his apprenticeship.

A colonial dyer added color to clothing.

The Tradesmen

Tradesmen built wheels and barrels. They shoed horses, tanned leather, and made tools. Some boys spent a number of years as an **apprentice** to a tradesman. Apprentices learned the skills to get jobs of their own. Maryland had few towns. Tradesmen often found jobs on plantations. Other people started new types of businesses. Ironwork in factories became important after 1715.

Colony Childhood

Doing their chores was one of the most important tasks of Maryland children. So was getting an education. Maryland did not build public schoolhouses. Families were scattered throughout the area. It would have been difficult to get enough students to fill a schoolroom. Most children received basic lessons in reading and writing at home. Rich families often sent their children to small private schools or to schools in England.

Adult family members were sometimes the only teachers colonial children had.

A wealthy Annapolis family welcomes visitors to its home.

Years of War

Maryland had become a thriving colony by the mid-1700s. The rich planters had stately brick mansions and expensive British-made clothes. Some had seats in the Maryland Assembly. A class of merchants took charge of trading Maryland products for goods made in Great Britain or elsewhere. Many small farmers had money to purchase silverware, books, and other useful items.

Wealthy colonists modeled their architecture and lifestyles after British fashion.

Maryland Politics

The Maryland Assembly was the lower house of the colony's two-house legislature. Wealthy planters controlled the assembly. Maryland's colony charter gave it some freedom from British control. But all laws passed by colonial legislatures still had to follow with British law. Wealthy colonists viewed themselves as British-style gentlemen. Pro-British feeling was strong.

Only men could vote for or become representatives in the colonial assembly.

Native Americans sometimes attacked frontier settlers in order to defend their own territory.

The Piedmont

German immigrants led the settlement of the Piedmont. This expanded Maryland's control of the region. Maize and other grains were the main crops. Lumber was also profitable. Most Germans worked small family farms. They had no need for enslaved workers. Many Germans also opposed slavery on religious grounds. The practice had less impact in the Piedmont than elsewhere. But the Piedmont frontier became a dangerous place in the 1750s.

During the French and Indian War, George Washington was promoted to the rank of major.

French and Indian War

Virginia **militia** under George Washington clashed with French soldiers in western Pennsylvania in 1754. The battle touched off the French and Indian War. This war was also called the Seven Years' War. It was the latest in a series of conflicts between France and Britain for control of North America. A larger French force soon drove the Virginians into Maryland. They built Fort Cumberland there. The Maryland Assembly organized a militia to guard the frontier against Indian groups supporting the French.

British troops under General Edward Braddock joined 450 colonists from Maryland and Virginia to force the French from western Pennsylvania. But an unexpected encounter with enemy forces turned it into a huge British defeat. The British army was too weakened to protect the frontier. Native Americans began to raid Maryland. Families fled east to escape. Britain defeated France in 1760. But Native Americans continued to attack British frontier forts to keep colonists out of their lands.

Though the British eventually won against the French, the financial cost and loss of life was difficult to overcome.

Price of Victory

King George III and
Parliament, Britain's
legislature, believed
the colonists should
help pay for the
war debts and the
frontier forts.
Parliament taxed
products such as sugar
and coffee in 1764
to raise money. The

**George III became king of Great
Britain in 1760.**

Stamp Act of 1765 forced colonists to buy a stamp
for printed materials such as legal documents and
magazines. This angered the colonists because
they did not have any representatives in the British
government to vote on the taxes.

The symbol
for the Sons of
Liberty was the
Liberty Tree. ➡

LIBERTY TREE

AN APPEAL TO GOD

Marylanders formed into groups such as the Sons of Liberty to protest what they called "taxation without representation." American colonists refused to buy British goods. Parliament ended the Stamp Act when British merchants complained about lost sales in the colonies. Britain passed more taxes in 1767. Parliament eventually dropped these as well, except for the tax on tea. A 1773 law favoring British tea merchants over American merchants added to the bad feelings.

Annapolis, Maryland, held its own tea party protest one month after Boston's.

Annapolis colonists burned the British ship the *Peggy Stewart* and its cargo of tea in 1774.

Rumblings of War

A Sons of Liberty group boarded British ships and threw hundreds of chests of tea into Boston Harbor on December 16, 1773. The British government closed the harbor in response. In September 1774, 12 American colonies sent **delegates** to a Continental Congress in Philadelphia. They discussed a response to Britain's actions. Some delegates wanted independence from Britain. Others hoped for a more peaceful solution.

In Maryland, rich planters and merchants led the pro-independence **Patriot** movement against Britain's control of the colonies. A group of men representing various parts of Maryland formed an unofficial

Sir Robert Eden was the last royal governor of Maryland.

government weeks after the First Continental Congress met. The colony's governor recognized that he had lost his power. He left office. Britain and the colonies inched closer to war the next April when British troops fought Massachusetts militiamen at Lexington and Concord.

The Second Continental Congress chose George Washington to command the newly formed Continental army in 1775. More delegates began to support the idea of independence from Britain as fighting continued. Some Maryland towns and the Piedmont Germans raised militias. The Declaration of Independence officially broke the colonies' bond with Britain on July 4, 1776. Marylanders quickly created a new state government by writing a **constitution**.

George Washington greets his new troops in Cambridge, Massachusetts.

The Maryland 400

On August 27, 1776, 400 Maryland troops fought in the Battle of Long Island in New York. The outnumbered Marylanders held the line all day against British attacks. Enemy troops finally swarmed the Continental army from three sides. The colonials retreated across a marsh. Lord Stirling was the American commander. He kept 250 Maryland soldiers with him to hold off the British. The Marylanders charged the thousands of enemy troops six times while the rest of the Continentals escaped.

Marylanders in the War

German immigrants from the Piedmont fought in the Continental army in New Jersey and Pennsylvania. They spent a freezing winter at Valley Forge, Pennsylvania, in 1777 with poor clothing and little food. John Eager Howard of Baltimore

John Eager Howard was a successful officer during the war. He later served as a senator and governor of Maryland.

led troops at the Battle of Cowpens. It was a stunning American victory that turned the war in the Continentals' favor. Maryland slaves fought for both sides. Those in the Continental army earned their freedom by serving.

Britain's main forces surrendered to the Americans after they were defeated at the Battle of Yorktown in October 1781. The Continental Congress approved a peace treaty with Britain in 1783. But the victorious Americans faced many problems. The Continental Congress owed money to other countries that helped fight the war, such as France and Spain. The colonists also could not agree on the next steps to take as a new, independent nation.

In 1783, Washington resigned as the Continental commander at the Maryland State House.

Maryland's Founding Fathers

The Second Continental Congress met in Philadelphia on May 10, 1775. The five Maryland delegates represented a colony split between those who wanted independence and others who desired to remain attached to Great Britain. After long debate, delegates from all the colonies voted on July 2, 1776, to break away from Britain. Four Marylanders signed the Declaration of Independence. One of them, Thomas Stone, left politics shortly afterward.

Charles Carroll

Charles Carroll was the only Catholic to sign the declaration. He had to fight religious prejudice in Maryland to enter politics. Carroll was one of America's richest men. He used part of his money to aid the colonials during the Revolutionary War. Carroll lived to age 95. He was the last signer of the declaration to die.

Samuel Chase

Samuel Chase was a former member of the Sons of Liberty. He served in the Continental Congress from 1774 to 1778. The fiery Chase battled political opponents his entire adult life. He was thrown out of a debating club in Annapolis. He also narrowly avoided being removed from the U.S. Supreme Court in 1805.

William Paca

William Paca was a friend and ally of Chase. He practiced law and cofounded his county's chapter of the Sons of Liberty. Paca served as Maryland's governor and as a U.S. District Court judge for Maryland after the war.

Delegates met in 1787 to create a U.S. Constitution to govern the new nation. Maryland approved it on April 26, 1788. Much had changed since the first settlers arrived. The population had grown to about 320,000. About one-third of these were enslaved people. Baltimore had become a large harbor city. Maryland would continue to grow and change as part of a new country. ★

Baltimore served as the nation's capital for a few months from 1776 to 1777.

Baltimore continued to grow into a successful harbor town in the 1800s and beyond.

True Statistics

Length of a dugout canoe: 20 ft. (6.1 m)

Length of service for an indentured servant: 5 to 7 years

Number of Maryland men for each woman in the colony in the mid-1600s: About 3 to 1

Size of Maryland's slave population in 1715: 8,000

Age of Charles Carroll when he died: 95

Number of houses in the Maryland Assembly: 2

Year Continental Congress approved a peace treaty with Britain: 1783

Number of Marylanders covering the retreat at the Battle of Long Island: 250

Population of Maryland in 1788: 320,000

A LAW
of
MARYLAND
Concerning
RELIGION.

Did you find the truth?

(F) Slavery was illegal in Maryland.

(T) Tobacco was a major crop in colonial Maryland.

Resources

Books

Ingram, Scott. *Battle of Long Island*. San Diego: Blackbirch, 2004.

Jensen, Niels R. *Maryland*. Edina, MN: ABDO, 2010.

Johnston, Joyce. *Maryland*. Minneapolis: Lerner, 2003.

Levy, Debbie. *Maryland*. San Diego: KidHaven, 2004.

Lusted, Marcia A. *Maryland: The Old Line State*. New York: PowerKids Press, 2010.

Santella, Andrew. *The French and Indian War*. Mankato, MN: Compass Point, 2004.

Somervill, Barbara A. *Maryland*. New York: Children's Press, 2009.

Stefoff, Rebecca. *Colonial Life*. New York: Benchmark, 2003.

Organizations and Web Sites

Maryland Historical Society

www.mdhs.org/explore

Look at online exhibits of objects dating from colonial to modern times.

Maryland State Archives

www.msa.md.gov

Examine a special collection of Maryland maps dating back to colonial times.

Places to Visit

Historic St. Mary's City

18751 Hogaboom Lane
St. Mary's City, MD 20686
(301) 475-4411
www.stmaryscity.org
Explore an outdoor museum and watch reenactments of great moments in Maryland history on the site of Maryland's first capital.

William Paca House

186 Prince George Street
Annapolis, MD 21401
(410) 267-7619
www.hometownannapolis.
com/tour_paca.html
Experience colonial Maryland by touring the house and gardens of William Paca, a signer of the Declaration of Independence.

Important Words

Algonquian (al-GON-kwin) — a group of Native American peoples that once lived across eastern North America

apprentice (uh-PREN-tis) — a person who learns a skill by working with an expert

cash crop (KASH KROP) — a crop grown for sale rather than for a family's own use

charter (CHAHR-tur) — a formal document guaranteeing rights or privileges

constitution (kahn-sti-TOO-shun) — the laws of a country that state the rights of the people and the powers of government

delegates (DEL-i-gitz) — representatives to a convention or congress

immigrants (IM-uh-gruhntz) — people who move from one country to another and settle there permanently

indentured servants (in-DEHN-shurd SUR-ventz) — people who agreed to work a certain amount of time in return for paid transportation to the colonies

legislature (LEJ-is-lay-chur) — a group of people who have the power to make or change laws

militia (muh-LISH-uh) — a group of people who are trained to fight but who aren't professional soldiers

Patriot (PAY-tree-uht) — an American colonist opposed to Great Britain

Index

Page numbers in **bold** indicate illustrations

About the Author

Kevin Cunningham has written more than 40 books on disasters, the history of disease, Native Americans, and other topics. Cunningham lives near Chicago with his wife and young daughter.